1,000
Japanese Words

タコ
tako
octopus

Berlitz Kids™
Berlitz Publishing/APA Publications GmbH & Co. Verlag KG
Singapore Branch, Singapore

Contacting the Editors
Every effort has been made to provide accurate information in this publication, but changes are inevitable. The publisher cannot be responsible for any resulting loss, inconvenience or injury. We would appreciate it if readers would call our attention to any errors or outdated information by contacting Apa Publications, 38 Joo Koon Road, Singapore 628990. Fax: (65) 6861 6438, E-mail: susan@apasin.com.sg

Table of Contents

かぞく **kazoku**
The family

おじさん **ojisan** uncle

おとうさん **otoosan** dad

おかあさん **okaasan** mom

おばさん **obasan** aunt

ほほえむ **hohoemu** to smile

カメラ **kamera** camera

あかちゃん **akachan** baby

おじいさん **ojiisan** grandpa

おばあさん **obaasan** grandma

むすこ **musuko** son

むすめ **musume** daughter

いぬ **inu** dog

おとこのひと
otokono-hito
man

おんなのひと
onnano-hito
woman

ネックレス
nekkuresu
necklace

ブレスレット
buresuretto
bracelet

おっと
otto
husband

つま
tsuma
wife

あごひげ
agohige
beard

うでどけい
udedokei
watch

ゆびわ
yubiwa
ring

だきしめる
dakishimeru
to hug

おねえさん（いもうと）
oneesan (imooto)
elder sister (younger sister)

おとうと（おにいさん）
otooto (oniisan)
younger brother (elder brother)

おんなのこ
onnano-ko
girl

こいぬ
koinu
puppy

こねこ
koneko
kitten

おとこのこ
otokono-ko
boy

5

キッチンで kicchinde
In the kitchen

さら
sara
dishes

でんわ
denwa
telephone

オーブン
oobun
oven

でんしレンジ
denshi-renji
microwave oven

しょっきだな
shokkidana
cupboard

ローストする
roosut-o-suru
to roast

やく
yaku
to bake

エプロン
epuron
apron

さらをあらう
sara-o-arau
to wash the dishes

ミルク
miruku
milk

まぜる
mazeru
to mix

こぼす
kobosu
to spill

ボール
booru
bowl

さとう
satoo
sugar

けいりょうカップ
keiryoo-kappu
measuring cup

こむぎこ
komugiko
flour

はちみつ
hachimitsu
honey

6

なべ
nabe
pot

フライパン
furai-pan
frying pan

こげた
kogeta
burnt

クッキー
kukkii
cookie

トースター
toosutaa
toaster

トースト
toosuto
toast

フリーザー
furiizaa
freezer

りょうりする
ryoori-suru
to cook

においをかぐ
nioi-o-kagu
to smell

チーズ
chiizu
cheese

ふっとうする
futtoo-suru
to boil

オレンジジュース
orenji-jyuusu
orange juice

たまご
tamago
egg

たべもの
tabemono
food

コンロ
konro
stove

バター
bataa
butter

れいぞうこ
reizooko
refrigerator

7

リビングで **ribingu-de**
In the living room

え
e
picture

しゃしん
shashin
photograph

ドア
doa
door

ヘッドフォン
heddofon
headphones

ＣＤプレーヤー
shiidii-pureeyaa
CD player

うたう
utau
to sing

ピアノ
piano
piano

ピアノをひく
piano-o-hiku
to play

カセットプレーヤー
kasetto-pureeyaa
tape player

カセットテープ
kasetto-teepu
cassette tape

CD
shiidii
compact disk

ラップトップ
rappu-toppu
laptop

かびん
kabin
vase

カーテン
kaaten
curtain

とりかご
torikago
birdcage

しょくぶつ
shokubutsu
plant

ねこ
neko
cat

テレビ
terebi
television

ほんだな
hondana
book shelf

ビデオプレーヤ
bideo-pureeyaa
VCR

コーヒーテーブル
koohii-teeburu
coffee table

しんぶん
shinbun
newspaper

ランプ
ranpu
lamp

ソファ
sofaa
couch

ひじかけいす
hijikake-isu
chair

ざっし
zasshi
magazine

カーペット
kaapetto
carpet

ベッドルームで
beddoruumu-de
In the bedroom

ポスター
posutaa
poster

つくえ
tsukue
desk

スリッパ
surippa
slipper

にんぎょう
ningyoo
doll

いす
isu
chair

てんとう
tentou
on

パジャマ
pajama
pajamas

おんがく
ongaku
music

でんきスタンド
denki-sutando
light

ラジオ
rajio
radio

ようふくだんす
yoofuku-dansu
dresser

もうふ
moofu
blanket

シーツ
shiitsu
sheet

ぬいぐるみ
nuigurumi
stuffed animal

かべ
kabe
wall

でんげんスイッチ
dengensuicchi
light switch

ハンガー
hangaa
clothes hanger

おしいれ
oshiire
closet

まど
mado
window

まんがほん
manga-hon
comic book

しょうとう
shoutou
off

おもちゃ
omocha
toys

くつした
kutsushita
sock

めざましどけい
mezamashi-dokei
alarm clock

ひきだし
hikidashi
drawer

ねる
neru
to sleep

ベッド
beddo
bed

まくら
makura
pillow

11

バスルームで basuruumu-de
In the bathroom

やくひんとだな
yakuhin-todana
medicine cabinet

くし
kushi
comb

かがみ
kagami
mirror

こうすい
koosui
perfume

でんきかみそり
denki-kamisori
electric razor

はぶらし
haburashi
toothbrush

はをみがく
haomigaku
to brush your teeth

せっけん
sekken
soap

せんめんタオル
senmen-taoru
washcloth

ながし
nagashi
sink

はみがきこ
hamigakiko
toothpaste

あらう
arau
to wash

バスローブ
basuroobu
bathrobe

ゆか
yuka
floor

かわかす
kawakasu
to dry

きれいにする
kireinisuru
clean

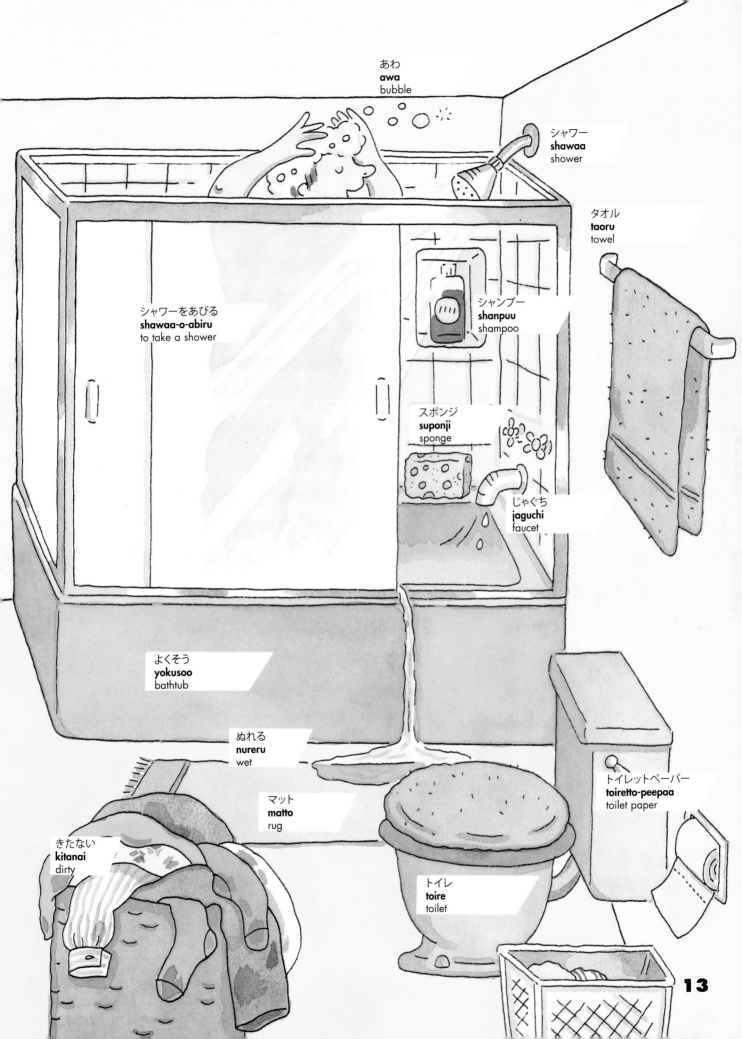

あわ
awa
bubble

シャワー
shawaa
shower

タオル
taoru
towel

シャワーをあびる
shawaa-o-abiru
to take a shower

シャンプー
shanpuu
shampoo

スポンジ
suponji
sponge

じゃぐち
jaguchi
faucet

よくそう
yokusoo
bathtub

ぬれる
nureru
wet

マット
matto
rug

トイレットペーパー
toiretto-peepaa
toilet paper

きたない
kitanai
dirty

トイレ
toire
toilet

13

さぎょうばで
sagyouba-de
In the workshop

かぎあな
kagiana
lock

くまで
kumade
rake

ドリル
doriru
drill

あな
ana
hole

ネジ
neji
screw

かいだん
kaidan
stairs

うえきばち
ueki-bachi
flowerpot

しゃりん
sharin
wheel

しゅうりする
shuurisuru
to repair

じてんしゃ
jitensha
bicycle

プライヤー
puraiyaa
pliers

なんきんじょう
nankinjoo
padlock

かぎ
kagi
key

どうぐばこ
dougubako
toolbox

14

15

たんじょうかい **tanjyookai**
The birthday party

あげる
ageru
to give

ダンスする
dansu-suru
to dance

ゲーム
geemu
game

ふうせん
fuusen
balloon

ナイフ
naifu
knife

さいころ
saikoro
dice

さら
sara
plate

キャンディ
kyandee
candy

スプーン
supuun
spoon

フォーク
fooku
fork

16

ビデオカメラ
bideo-kamera
video camera

ろうそく
roosoku
candle

ふく
fuku
to blow

ケーキ
keeki
cake

たんじょうびカード
tanjoobi-kaado
birthday card

リボン
ribon
bow

プレゼント
purezento
present

ほほえむ
hohoemu
smile

あける
akeru
to open

リボン
ribon
ribbon

つつみをあける
tsutsumi-o-akeru
to unwrap

つつみがみ
tsutsumi-gami
wrapping paper

17

ショッピングセンターで
shoppingu-senntaa-de
At the shopping center

みぎ
migi
right

うる
uru
to sell

ひだり
hidari
left

スニーカー
suniikaa
sneaker

くつ
kutsu
shoe

おつり
otsuri
change

ジッパーをあげる
jippaa-o-ageru
to zip up

おかね
okane
money

ドレス
doresu
dress

かう
kau
to buy

ブラウス
burausu
blouse

ハンドバッグ
handobaggu
purse

ねだん
nedan
price

スカート
sukaato
skirt

18

ネクタイ
nekutai
tie

ぼうし
booshi
hat

スーツ
suutsu
suit

ベルト
beruto
belt

さいふ
saifu
wallet

めがね
megane
glasses

ポケット
poketto
pocket

ジーンズ
jiinzu
jeans

うえ
ue
up

した
shita
down

てんいん
tenin
store clerk

おきゃくさん
okyakusann
customer

しちゃくする
shichaku-suru
to try on

ズボン
zubon
pants

ティシャツ
T-shatsu
T-shirt

バーゲン
baagen
bargain

はんズボン
han-zubon
shorts

シャツ
shatsu
shirt

19

スーパーマーケットで
suupaa-maaketto-de
At the supermarket

たまねぎ
tamanegi
onion

レタス
retasu
lettuce

すいか
suika
watermelon

トマト
tomato
tomato

キャベツ
kyabetsu
cabbage

なし
nashi
pear

レモン
remon
lemon

プラム
puramu
plum

オレンジ
orenji
orange

カリフラワー
karifurawaa
cauliflower

ブロッコリ
burokkori
broccoli

りんご
ringo
apple

バナナ
banana
banana

ニンニク
ninniku
garlic

セロリ
serori
celery

ピーマン
piiman
green pepper

ぶどう
budoo
grape

パイナップル
painappuru
pineapple

さくらんぼ
sakuranbo
cherry

にんじん
ninjin
carrot

やさい
yasai
vegetable

フルーツ
furuutsu
fruit

はらう
harau
to pay

さかな
sakana
fish

にく
niku
meat

ヨーグルト
yooguruto
yogurt

まめ
mame
bean

たな
tana
shelf

つうろ
tsuuro
aisle

シリアル
shiriaru
cereal

こめ
kome
rice

ショッピングカート
shoppinngu-kaato
shopping cart

ふくろ
fukuro
bag

21

レストランで
resutoran-de
In the restaurant

パン
pan
bread

つまずく
tsumazuku
to trip

スパゲッティ
supagettii
spaghetti

とりにく
toriniku
chicken

おなかがすく
onakagasuku
to be hungry

ゆうしょく
yuushoku
dinner

ボトル
botoru
bottle

テーブル
teeburu
table

ウエートレス
ueetoresu
waitress

クラッカー
kurakkaa
cracker

あつい
atsui
hot

のむ
nomu
to drink

コップ
koppu
glass

サラダ
sarada
salad

ナプキン
napukin
napkin

スープ
suupu
soup

みず
mizu
water

テーブルクロス
teeburu-kurosu
tablecloth

コーヒー
koohii
coffee

デザート
dezaato
dessert

わける
wakeru
to share

そそぐ
sosogu
to pour

メニュー
menyuu
menu

カップ
kappu
cup

ウエイター
ueitaa
waiter

こしょう
koshoo
pepper

たべる
taberu
to eat

かける
kakeru
to put

きる
kiru
to cut

しお
shio
salt

ピザ
piza
pizza

23

きょうしつで **kyooshitsu-de**
In the classroom

けいじばん
keijiban
bulletin board

のり
nori
glue

ほん
hon
book

コンピューター
konpyuutaa
computer

クレヨン
kureyon
crayon

カレンダー
karendaa
calendar

ペン
pen
pen

じしょ
jisho
dictionary

よむ
yomu
to read

せんせい
sensei
teacher

すうじ
suuji
number

しゅくだい
shukudai
homework

せいと
seito
student

24

こくばん
kokuban
chalkboard

さんすう
sansuu
math

わる
waru
to divide

かける
kakeru
to multiply

たす
tasu
to add

ひく
hiku
to subtract

かんがえる
kangaeru
to think

ちきゅうぎ
chikyuugi
globe

こくばんけし
kokuban-keshi
eraser

チョーク
chooku
chalk

マーカー
maakaa
marker

ホチキス
hochikisu
stapler

おしえる
oshieru
to teach

しつもんする
shitsumon-suru
to ask

けいさんき
keisanki
calculator

えんぴついれ
enpitsu-ire
pencil case

ノート
nooto
notebook

えんぴつ
enpitsu
pencil

えんぴつけずり
enpitsu-kezuri
pencil sharpener

らんどせる
randoseru
backpack

どうぶつえんで
doobutsuen-de
At the zoo

かるい
karui
light

おもい
omoi
heavy

かば
kaba
hippopotamus

ワニ
wani
crocodile

ワニ
wani
alligator

ぞう
zoo
elephant

ガイド
gaido
guide

つよい
tsuyoi
strong

ゴリラ
gorira
gorilla

ぶらさがる
burasagaru
to hang

とどく
todoku
to reach

かく
kaku
to scratch

のぼる
noboru
to climb

さる
saru
monkeys

チンパンジー
chinpanjii
chimpanzee

シロクマ
shirokuma
polar bear

ヒョウ
hyoo
leopard

くま
kuma
bear

どうぶつえんのしいくがかり
doobutsuen-no-shiikugakari
zoo keeper

サイ
sai
rhinoceros

しっぽ
shippo
tail

つの
tsuno
horn

トラ
tora
tiger

しゃしんをとる
shashin-o-toru
to take photos

シマウマ
shimauma
zebra

ほえる
hoeru
to roar

(おす)ライオン
(osu)raion
lion

どうぶつ
doobutsu
animal

ガゼル
gazeru
gazelle

キリン
kirin
giraffe

(めす)ライオン
(mesu)raion
lioness

ライオンのこ
raionnoko
cub

だちょう
dachoo
ostrich

27

こうえんで **kooen-de**
In the park

ピクニックバスケット
pikunikku-basuketto
picnic basket

かくれんぼをする
kakurenbo-o-suru
to play hide and seek

アリ
ari
ant

ポテトチップス
poteto-chippusu
potato chips

レモネード
remoneedo
lemonade

リス
risu
squirrel

ピクニック
pikunikku
picnic

サンドイッチ
sandoicchi
sandwich

ピクニックテーブル
pikunikku-teeburu
picnic table

とりごや
torigoya
birdhouse

きのみ
kinomi
nut

くしゃみをする
kushami-o-suru
to sneeze

しげみ
shigemi
bush

とおり
toori
path

ローラースケート
rooraa-sukeeto
roller skates

たこ
tako
kite

ブランコにのる
buranko-ni-noru
to swing

あそびば
asobiba
playground

ブランコ
buranko
swing

すべりだい
suberidai
slide

なわとびをする
nawatobi-o-suru
to jump rope

ふんすい
funsui
fountain

シーソー
shiisoo
see-saw

すなば
sunaba
sandbox

フリスビー
furisubii
Frisbee®

ほえる
hoeru
to bark

くさ
kusa
grass

ヘルメット
herumetto
helmet

スケートボード
sukeetoboodo
skateboard

インラインスケート
inrainsukeeto
in-line skates

29

ゆうえんちで yuuenchi-de
At the amusement park

サーカス
saakasu
circus

ローラーコースター
rooraa-koosutaa
roller coaster

ピエロ
piero
clown

てじなし
tejinashi
magician

めまいがする
memaigasuru
dizzy

おばけ
obake
ghost

あいのとんねる
ainotonneru
tunnel of love

ハート
haato
heart

モンスター
monsutaa
monster

おばけやしき
obakeyashiki
haunted house

コンサート
konsaato
concert

かしゅ
kashu
singer

スピーカー
supiikaa
loudspeakers

マイク
maiku
microphone

たかい
takai
high

かんらんしゃ
kanransha
Ferris wheel

ひくい
hikui
low

まと
mato
target

ゆみ
yumi
bow

や
ya
arrow

あやつりにんぎょう
ayatsuri-ningyoo
puppet

メリーゴーランド
merii-goo-rando
carousel

わたあめ
wataame
cotton candy

チケット
chiketto
ticket

れつ
retsu
line

31

びょういんで **byooin-de**
In the hospital

くすり
kusuri
medicine

いしゃ
isha
doctor

かんごふ
kangofu
(female) nurse

くるまいす
kurumaisu
wheelchair

きゅうきゅうしゃ
kyuukyuusha
ambulance

エレベーター
erebeetaa
elevator

ギブス
gibusu
cast

ストレッチャー
sutorecchaa
stretcher

ほうたい
hootai
bandage

いしゃ
isha
doctor

レントゲンしゃしん
rentogen-shashin
x-ray

かんごし
kangoshi
(male) nurse

びょうきになる
byooki-ni-naru
to be sick

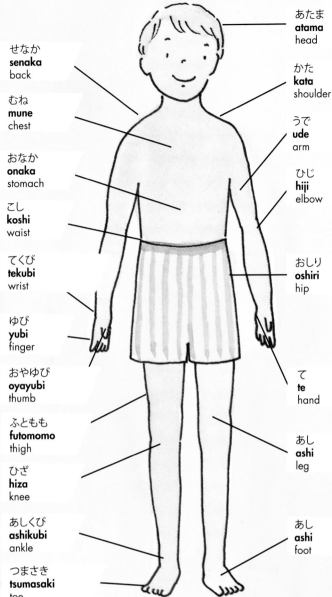

せなか
senaka
back

むね
mune
chest

おなか
onaka
stomach

こし
koshi
waist

てくび
tekubi
wrist

ゆび
yubi
finger

おやゆび
oyayubi
thumb

ふともも
futomomo
thigh

ひざ
hiza
knee

あしくび
ashikubi
ankle

つまさき
tsumasaki
toe

あたま
atama
head

かた
kata
shoulder

うで
ude
arm

ひじ
hiji
elbow

おしり
oshiri
hip

て
te
hand

あし
ashi
leg

あし
ashi
foot

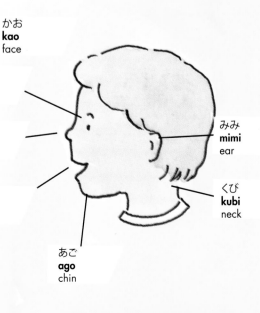

かお
kao
face

め
me
eye

はな
hana
nose

くち
kuchi
mouth

みみ
mimi
ear

くび
kubi
neck

あご
ago
chin

33

はくぶつかんで
hakubutsukan-de
At the museum

ほし
hoshi
star

ちきゅう
chikyuu
Earth

ロケット
roketto
rocket

うちゅうひこうし
uchuu-hikooshi
astronaut

しろ
shiro
white

つき
tsuki
moon

けいびいん
keibiin
guard

ちゃいろ
chairo
brown

きょうりゅう
kyooryuu
dinosaur

がいこつ
gaikotsu
skeleton

みずいろ
mizuiro
light blue

イラスト
irasuto
art

え
e
painting

むらさき
murasaki
purple

ピンク
pinku
pink

くろ
kuro
black

オレンジ
orenji
orange

あか
aka
red

みずたまもよう
mizutamamoyou
polka dots

しまもよう
shimamoyou
stripes

みどり
midori
green

こんいろ
kon-iro
dark blue

はいいろ
hai-iro
gray

ちょうこく
chookoku
sculpture

きいろ
ki-iro
yellow

でぐち
deguchi
exit

ピラミッド
piramiddo
pyramid

てんじかい
tenjikai
exhibit

いりぐち
iriguchi
entrance

ミイラ
miira
mummy

35

ビーチで **biichi-de**
At the beach

とうだい
toodai
lighthouse

しま
shima
island

なみ
nami
wave

サーフボード
saafuboodo
surfboard

しぶきをあげる
shibuki-o-ageru
to splash

すいちゅうメガネ
suichuu-megane
diving mask

スノーケル
sunookeru
snorkel

フィン
fin
fins

およぐ
oyogu
to swim

ボール
booru
ball

ひやけどめローション
hiyakedome-rooshon
suntan lotion

リラックスする
rirakkusu-suru
to relax

のみもの
nomimono
drink

かいがら
kaigara
seashell

あそぶ
asobu
to play

みずでっぽう
mizu-deppoo
water gun

サンダル
sandaru
sandal

サングラス
sangurasu
sunglasses

クーラー
kuuraa
cooler

やしのき
yashinoki
palmtree

ヨット
yotto
sailboat

たいよう
taiyoo
sun

カモメ
kamome
seagull

ダイビングする
daibingu-suru
to dive

いわ
iwa
rock

すなのしろ
suna-no-shiro
sand castle

みずぎ
mizugi
swimsuit

すな
suna
sand

バケツ
baketsu
bucket

バレーボール
bareebooru
volleyball

かんしいん
kanshiin
lifeguard

ネット
netto
net

37

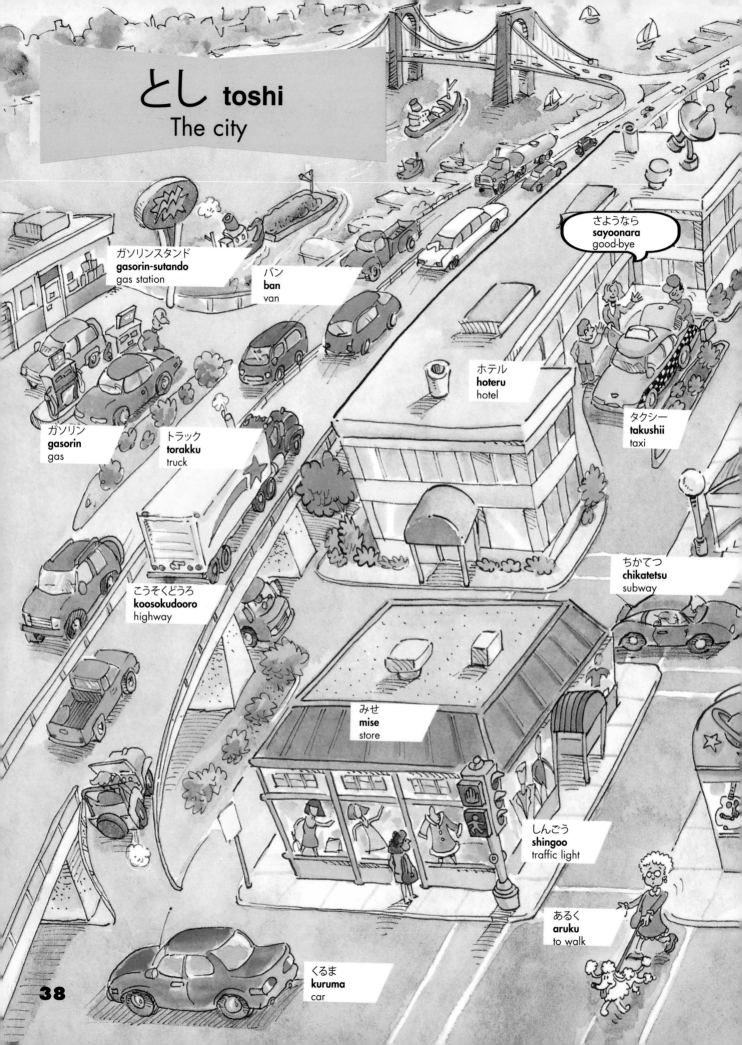

とし toshi
The city

ガソリンスタンド
gasorin-sutando
gas station

バン
ban
van

さようなら
sayoonara
good-bye

ホテル
hoteru
hotel

タクシー
takushii
taxi

ガソリン
gasorin
gas

トラック
torakku
truck

ちかてつ
chikatetsu
subway

こうそくどうろ
koosokudooro
highway

みせ
mise
store

しんごう
shingoo
traffic light

あるく
aruku
to walk

くるま
kuruma
car

まち machi
The town

やね
yane
roof

いえ
ie
house

しょくりょうひんてん
shokuryoohinten
grocery store

パレード
pareedo
parade

ゴミばこ
gomibako
garbage can

えをかく
e-o-kaku
to paint

えふで
efude
paintbrush

がか
gaka
painter

は
ha
tooth

はいしゃ
haisha
dentist

ハサミ
hasami
scissors

とこや
tokoya
barbershop

さんぱつ
sanpatsu
haircut

とこやさん
tokoyasan
barber

40

はた **hata** flag

のうか **nouka** town hall

ゆうびんきょく **yuubinkyoku** post office

てがみ **tegami** letter

バンド **bando** band

ポスト **posuto** mailbox

とまる **tomaru** to stop

バイク **baiku** motorcycle

ベンチ **benchi** bench

アイスクリーム **aisukuriimu** ice cream

チョコレート **chokoreeto** chocolate

バニラ **banira** vanilla

いちご **ichigo** strawberry

えいがかん **eigakan** movie theater

えいが **eiga** movie

アイスクリームや **aisukuriimu-ya** ice cream shop

41

いなか **inaka**
The countryside

くもり
kumori
cloudy

かみなり
kaminari
lightning

あめがふる
amegafuru
to rain

あらし
arashi
storm

あめ
ame
rain

こや
koya
cabin

かぜ
kaze
wind

はっぱ
happa
leaf

かさ
kasa
umbrella

き
ki
tree

レインコート
reinkooto
raincoat

くも
kumo
cloud

にじ
niji
rainbow

やま
yama
mountain

トンネル
tonneru
tunnel

はし
hashi
bridge

でんしゃ
densha
train

ちょうちょ
choocho
butterfly

うさぎ
usagi
rabbit

かわ
kawa
river

きつね
kitsune
fox

おか
oka
hill

ぼくじょう
bokujyou
field

とり
tori
bird

はな
hana
flower

43

のうじょうで
noojoo-de
At the farm

ひつじかい
hitsujikai
shepherd

ひつじ
hitsuji
sheep

こひつじ
kohitsuji
lamb

ヤギ
yagi
goat

こうま
kouma
colt

うま
uma
horse

こうし
koushi
calf

おうし
oushi
bull

めうし
meushi
cow

さく
saku
fence

かえる
kaeru
frog

いど
ido
well

アヒル
ahiru
duck

いけ
ike
pond

ガチョウ
gachoo
goose

うまごや
umagoya
stable

ぶた
buta
pig

くら
kura
saddle

ほしぐさ
hoshigusa
hay

のる
noru
to ride

のうか
nooka
farmer

トラクター
torakutaa
tractor

かかし
kakashi
scarecrow

こむぎ
komugi
wheat

とうもろこし
toomorokoshi
corn

はたけ
hatake
garden

にわし
niwashi
gardener

ホース
hoosu
hose

なや
naya
barn

しちめんちょう
shichimenchoo
turkey

オンドリ
ondori
rooster

とりごや
torigoya
chicken coop

ねずみ
nezumi
mouse

たる
taru
barrel

メンドリ
mendori
hen

45

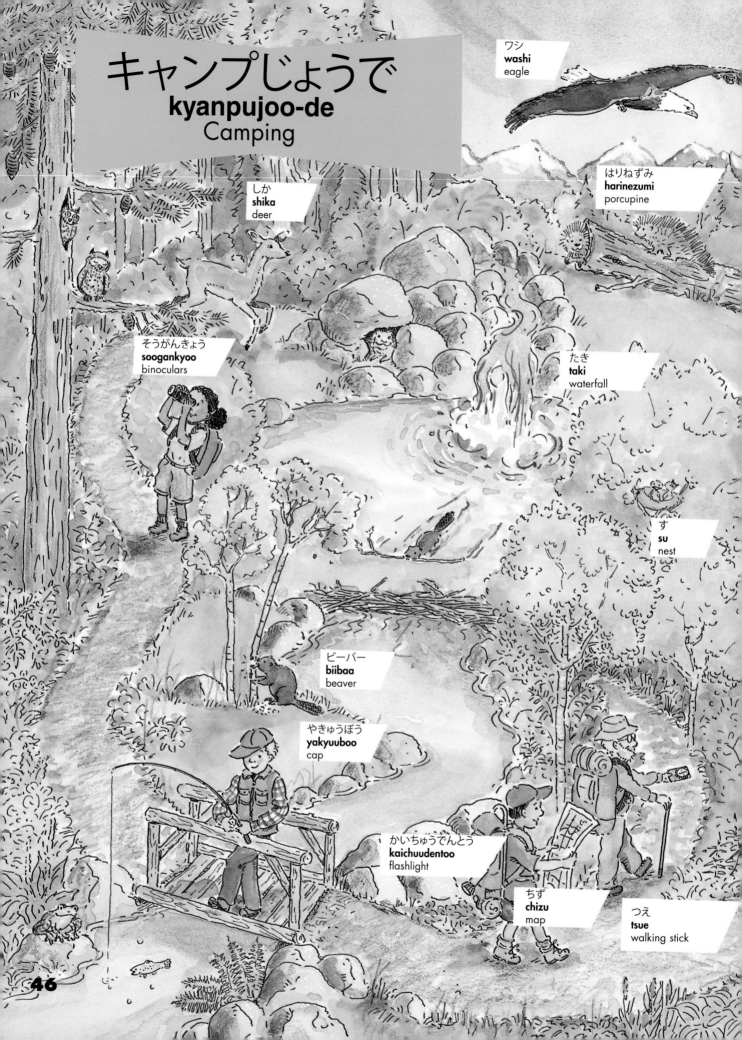

キャンプじょうで
kyanpujoo-de
Camping

ワシ
washi
eagle

しか
shika
deer

はりねずみ
harinezumi
porcupine

そうがんきょう
soogankyoo
binoculars

たき
taki
waterfall

す
su
nest

ビーバー
biibaa
beaver

やきゅうぼう
yakyuuboo
cap

かいちゅうでんとう
kaichuudentoo
flashlight

ちず
chizu
map

つえ
tsue
walking stick

テント
tento
tent

へび
hebi
snake

ねぶくろ
nebukuro
sleeping bag

けむり
kemuri
smoke

スカンク
sukanku
skunk

マッチ
macchi
matches

アライグマ
araiguma
raccoon

グリル
guriru
grill

キャンプファイヤー
kyanpu-faiyaa
campfire

とざんどう
tozandou
trail

ウィンタースポーツ
uintaa-supootsu
Winter sports

セーター
seetaa
sweater

おる
oru
to break

スキーをする
skii-o-suru
to ski

ゆき
yuki
snow

ころぶ
korobu
to fall

ゆきだるま
yukidaruma
snowman

ゴーグル
googuru
goggles

はくしゅする
hakushu-suru
to clap

ジャケット
jyaketto
jacket

スキー
sukii
skis

ブーツ
buutsu
boots

すこっぷ
sukoppu
shovel

さけぶ
sakubu
to shout

そり
sori
sled

グローブ
guroobu
gloves

スノーボード
sunooboodo
snowboard

スカーフ
sukaafu
scarf

てぶくろ
tebukuro
mittens

ゆきだま
yukudaruma
snowball

さむい
samui
to be cold

コート
kooto
coat

アイス
aisu
ice

ゴール
gooru
goal

ゴールキーパー
goorukiipaa
goalie

アイススケートをする
aisusukeeto-o-suru
to ice skate

ホッケーのスティック
hokkee-no-suthikku
hockey stick

アイススケート
aisusukeeto
ice skates

ホッケーせんしゅ
hokkee-senshu
hockey player

パック
pakku
puck

49

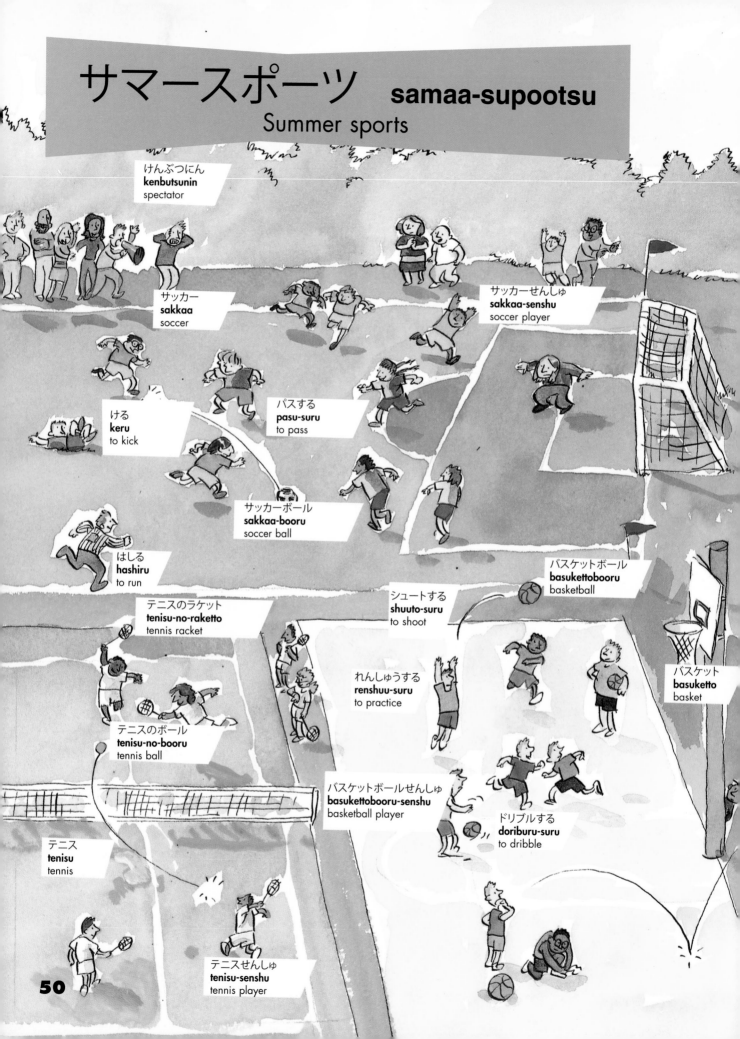

サマースポーツ samaa-supootsu
Summer sports

けんぶつにん
kenbutsunin
spectator

サッカー
sakkaa
soccer

サッカーせんしゅ
sakkaa-senshu
soccer player

ける
keru
to kick

パスする
pasu-suru
to pass

サッカーボール
sakkaa-booru
soccer ball

はしる
hashiru
to run

テニスのラケット
tenisu-no-raketto
tennis racket

シュートする
shuuto-suru
to shoot

バスケットボール
basukettobooru
basketball

れんしゅうする
renshuu-suru
to practice

バスケット
basuketto
basket

テニスのボール
tenisu-no-booru
tennis ball

バスケットボールせんしゅ
basukettobooru-senshu
basketball player

ドリブルする
doriburu-suru
to dribble

テニス
tenisu
tennis

テニスせんしゅ
tenisu-senshu
tennis player

50

とびこみだい
tobikomidai
diving board

きゅうめいぐ
kyuumeigu
life preserver

すいえいプール
suiei-puuru
swimming pool

やきゅう
yakyuu
baseball

なげる
nageru
to throw

キャッチする
kyacchi-suru
to catch

うつ
utsu
to hit

やきゅうのバット
yakyuu-no-batto
baseball bat

やきゅうのグローブ
yakyuu-no-guroobu
baseball glove

コーチ
koochi
coach

ベース
beesu
base

チーム
chiimu
team

やきゅうのせんしゅ
yakyuu-no-senshu
baseball player

うみ umi
The ocean

セイウチ
seiuchi
walrus

くじら
kujira
whale

アザラシ
azarashi
seal

クラゲ
kurage
jelly fish

イカ
ika
squid

せんすいかん
sensuikan
submarine

カメ
kame
turtle

サメ
same
shark

さかな
sakana
fish

ハマグリ
hamaguri
clam

サンゴ
sango
coral

ひらく
hiraku
open

とじる
tojiru
closed

ヒトデ
hitode
starfish

52

イルカ
iruka
dolphin

ひあたりのよい
hiatari-no-yoi
sunny

りょうし
ryooshi
fisherman

さかなつり
sakanatsuri
to fish

マグロ
maguro
tuna fish

ミミズ
mimizu
worm

タツノオトシゴ
tatsuno-otoshigo
seahorse

カニ
kani
crab

スキューバダイビングする
sukyuuba-daibingu-suru
to scuba dive

スキューバダイバー
sukyuuba-daibaa
scuba diver

メカジキ
mekajiki
swordfish

たから
takara
treasure

どうくつ
dookutsu
cave

ピカピカの
pikapika-no
shiny

ロブスター
robusutaa
lobster

タコ
tako
octopus

53

まほうのもりで mahoo-no-mori-de
In the enchanted forest

もり
mori
forest

ふくろう
fukuroo
owl

ほうき
hooki
broom

オオカミ
ookami
wolf

まじょ
majo
witch

ドラゴン
doragon
dragon

うつくしい
utsukushii
beautiful

ハンサム
hansamu
handsome

プリンス
purinsu
prince

プリンセス
purinsesu
princess

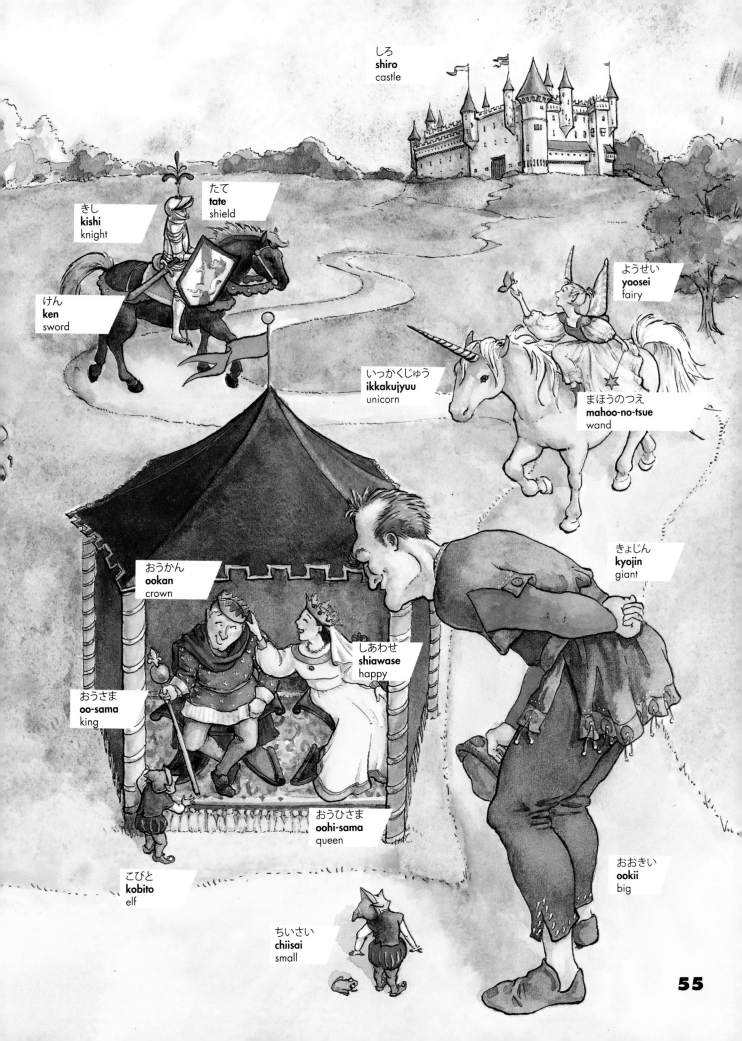

しろ
shiro
castle

たて
tate
shield

きし
kishi
knight

けん
ken
sword

ようせい
yoosei
fairy

いっかくじゅう
ikkakujyuu
unicorn

まほうのつえ
mahoo-no-tsue
wand

おうかん
ookan
crown

きょじん
kyojin
giant

しあわせ
shiawase
happy

おうさま
oo-sama
king

おうひさま
oohi-sama
queen

こびと
kobito
elf

ちいさい
chiisai
small

おおきい
ookii
big

55

りょこう **ryookoo**
Travel

りょこうする
ryokoo-suru
to travel

クルーズせん
kuruuzu-sen
cruise ship

パイロット
pairotto
pilot

くうこう
kuukoo
airport

ちゃくりくする
chakuriku-suru
to land

タグボート
tagu-booto
tugboat

スーツケース
suutsu-keesu
suitcase

ボート
booto
boat

ぜいかん
zeikan
customs

こうつう
kootsuu
traffic

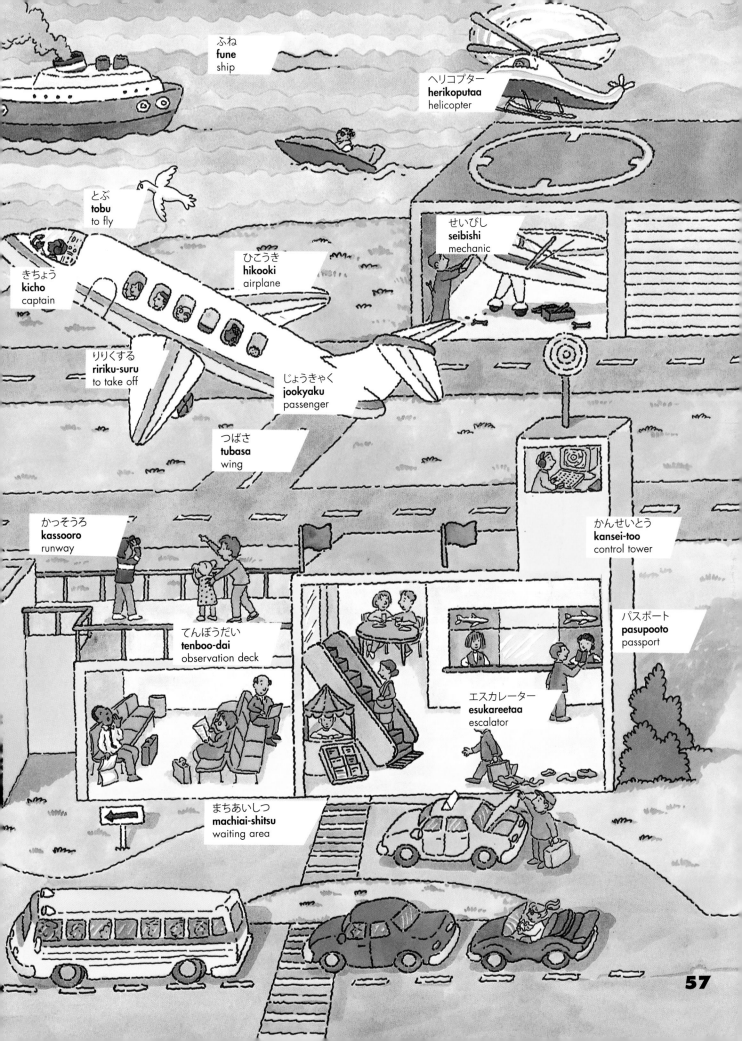

ふね **fune** ship

ヘリコプター **herikoputaa** helicopter

とぶ **tobu** to fly

せいびし **seibishi** mechanic

きちょう **kicho** captain

ひこうき **hikooki** airplane

りりくする **ririku-suru** to take off

じょうきゃく **jookyaku** passenger

つばさ **tubasa** wing

かんせいとう **kansei-too** control tower

かっそうろ **kassooro** runway

パスポート **pasupooto** passport

てんぼうだい **tenboo-dai** observation deck

エスカレーター **esukareetaa** escalator

まちあいしつ **machiai-shitsu** waiting area

そのた sonota
More Words

Words to describe	せつめいする たんご	setsumeisuru-tango	Nouns	めいし	meishi
angry	おこる	**okoru**	alphabet	アルファベット	**arufabetto**
bored	たいくつ	**taikutsu**	answer	こたえ	**kotae**
busy	いそがしい	**isogashii**	autumn	あき	**aki**
difficult	むずかしい	**muzukashii**	battery	でんち	**denchi**
easy	かんたん	**kantan**	bone	ほね	**hone**
hard	かたい	**katai**	bottom	そこ	**soko**
little	ちいさい	**chiisai**	box	はこ	**hako**
magenta	あかむらさきいろ	**akamurasaki-iro**	breakfast	あさごはん	**asa-gohan**
narrow	せまい	**semai**	candy bar	チョコバー	**chokobaa**
plaid	こうしじま	**kooshijima**	ceiling	てんじょう	**tenjoo**
quiet	しずか	**shizuka**	chapter	しょう	**shoo**
sad	かなしい	**kanashii**	circle	えん	**en**
short	みじかい	**mijikai**	clay	ねんど	**nendo**
straight	まっすぐ	**massugu**	clothes	ふく	**fuku**
tall	たかい	**takai**	color	いろ	**iro**
thick	あつい	**atsui**	cowboy	カウボーイ	**kau-booi**
thin	ほそい	**hosoi**	dining room	ダイニングルーム	**dainingu-ruumu**
tired	つかれた	**tsukareta**	end	おわり	**owari**
warm	あったかい	**attakai**	envelope	ふうとう	**fuutoo**
wide	ひろい	**hiroi**	grade	がくねん	**gakunen**
			guitar	ギター	**gitaa**
			gum	ガム	**gamu**
			heat	ねつ	**netsu**
			hero	ヒーロー	**hiiroo**
			lunch	ひるごはん	**hiru-gohan**

name	なまえ	**namae**	to have	もつ	**motsu**
peanut	ピーナッツ	**piinattsu**	to hear	きく	**kiku**
promise	やくそく	**yakusoku**	to kiss	キスする	**kisu-suru**
question	しつもん	**shitsumon**	to like	すき	**suki**
spring	はる	**haru**	to listen	きく	**kiku**
stamp	きって	**kitte**	to live	いきる	**ikiru**
staples	ホッチキス	**hocchikisu**	to love	あいする	**aisuru**
stool	ふみだい	**fumidai**	to make	つくる	**tsukuru**
story	ストーリー	**sutoorii**	to pull	ひく	**hiku**
summer	なつ	**natsu**	to push	おす	**osu**
surprise	おどろき	**odoroki**	to see	みる	**miru**
tea	おちゃ	**ocha**	to sew	ぬう	**nuu**
test	テスト	**tesuto**	to study	べんきょうする	**benkyoo-suru**
top	ちょうじょう	**choojoo**	to take	とる	**toru**
triangle	さんかく	**sankaku**	to tie	むすぶ	**musubu**
underwear	したぎ	**shitagi**	to touch	さわる	**sawaru**
vacation	バケーション	**bakeeshon**	to wake up	おきる	**okiru**
violin	バイオリン	**baiorin**	to want	ほしい	**hoshii**
winter	ふゆ	**fuyu**	to wave	ふる	**furu**
zipper	ジッパー	**jippaa**	to tie	むすぶ	**musubu**
			to wear	きる	**kiru**
			to whistle	くちぶえをふく	**kuchibue-o-fuku**

Verbs	どうし	**dooshi**	**Numbers**	すうじ	**suuji**
can	できる	**dekiru**	zero	ゼロ	**zero**
to build	たてる	**tateru**	one	いち	**ichi**
to close	とじる	**tojiru**	two	に	**ni**
to cry	なく	**naku**	three	さん	**san**
to do	する	**suru**	four	よん	**yon**
to draw	ひく	**hiku**	five	ご	**go**
to dream	ゆめをみる	**yume-o-miru**	six	ろく	**roku**
to guess	すいそくする	**suisoku-suru**	seven	しち	**shichi**

eight	はち	**hachi**		**Ordinal numbers**	じょすう	**josuu**
nine	きゅう	**kyuu**				
ten	じゅう	**jyuu**				
eleven	じゅういち	**jyuu-ichi**		first	ひとつめ	**hitotsu-me**
twelve	じゅうに	**jyuu-ni**		second	ふたつめ	**futatsu-me**
thirteen	じゅうさん	**jyuu-san**		third	みっつめ	**mittsu-me**
fourteen	じゅうよん	**jyuu-yon**		fourth	よっつめ	**yottsu-me**
fifteen	じゅうご	**jyuu-go**		fifth	いつつめ	**itsutsu-me**
sixteen	じゅうろく	**jyuu-roku**		sixth	むっつめ	**muttsu-me**
seventeen	じゅうしち	**jyuu-shichi**		seventh	ななつめ	**nanatsu-me**
eighteen	じゅうはち	**jyuu-hachi**		eighth	やっつめ	**yattsu-me**
nineteen	じゅうきゅう	**jyuu-kyuu**		ninth	ここのつめ	**kokonotsu-me**
twenty	にじゅう	**ni-jyuu**		tenth	じゅっこめ	**jyukko-me**
thirty	さんじゅう	**san-jyuu**				
forty	よんじゅう	**yon-jyuu**		**Days**	ようび	**yoobi**
fifty	ごじゅう	**go-jyuu**				
sixty	ろくじゅう	**roku-jyuu**		Sunday	にちようび	**nichi-yoobi**
seventy	ななじゅう	**nana-jyuu**		Monday	げつようび	**getsu-yoobi**
eighty	はちじゅう	**hachi-jyuu**		Tuesday	かようび	**ka-yoobi**
ninety	きゅうじゅう	**kyuu-jyuu**		Wednesday	すいようび	**sui-yoobi**
one hundred	ひゃく	**hyaku**		Thursday	もくようび	**moku-yoobi**
two hundred	にひゃく	**ni-hyaku**		Friday	きんようび	**kin-yoobi**
three hundred	さんびゃく	**san-byaku**		Saturday	どようび	**do-yoobi**
four hundred	よんひゃく	**yon-hyaku**				
five hundred	ごひゃく	**go-hyaku**		**Months**	つき	**tsuki**
six hundred	ろっぴゃく	**roppyaku**				
seven hundred	ななひゃく	**nana-hyaku**		January	いちがつ	**ichi-gatsu**
eight hundred	はっぴゃく	**happyaku**		February	にがつ	**ni-gatsu**
nine hundred	きゅうひゃく	**kyuu-hyaku**		March	さんがつ	**san-gatsu**
one thousand	せん	**sen**		April	しがつ	**shi-gatsu**
one million	ひゃくまん	**hyaku-man**		May	ごがつ	**go-gatsu**

June	ろくがつ	**roku-gatsu**
July	しちがつ	**shichi-gatsu**
August	はちがつ	**hachi-gatsu**
September	くがつ	**ku-gatsu**
October	じゅうがつ	**jyuu-gatsu**
November	じゅういちがつ	**jyuuichi-gatsu**
December	じゅうにがつ	**jyuuni-gatsu**

Elements of time	じかんの たんい	**jikanno-tan-i**
second	びょう	**byoo**
minute	ふん	**fun**
hour	じ	**ji**
day	にち	**nichi**
week	しゅう	**shuu**
month	つき	**tsuki**
year	ねん	**nen**
yesterday	きのう	**kinoo**
today	きょう	**kyoo**
tomorrow	あした	**ashita**
early	はやい	**hayai**
late	おそい	**osoi**

Useful words	べんりな たんご	**benrina-tango**
and	と	**to**
at	に	**ni**
between	あいだ	**aida**
but	でも	**demo**
he	かれ	**kare**

her	かのじょの	**kanojono**
hers	かのじょのもの	**kanojonomono**
his	かれのもの	**karenomono**
his	かれの	**kareno**
I	わたし	**watashi**
in	のなか	**no-naka**
it	それ	**sore**
its	その	**sono**
maybe	たぶん	**tabun**
mine	わたしのもの	**watashinomono**
Mr.	さま	**sama**
Mrs.	さま	**sama**
Ms.	さま	**sama**
my	わたしの	**watashino**
no	いいえ	**iie**
of	の	**no**
on	うえ	**ue**
our	わたしたちの	**watashitachino**
ours	わたしたちのもの	**watashitachino-mono**
outside	そと	**soto**
over	のうえ	**no-ue**
she	かのじょ	**kanojo**
their	かれらの	**karerano**
theirs	かれらのもの	**kareranomono**
they	かれら	**karera**
to	へ	**e**
under	した	**shita**
we	わたしたち	**watashitachi**
with	いっしょ	**issho**
yes	はい	**hai**

Index